DENMARK
- a kingdom

Dannebrog

Text and Photo: Robert Trojaborg
Translation: Compactas and Japanese Language Service
Distribution: Trojaborgs Forlag
                   Industrigrenen 4
                   2635 Ishøj
                   Danmark
                   Tlf. +45 43 54 58 00

                   ISBN 87-89868-02-1

                   1997

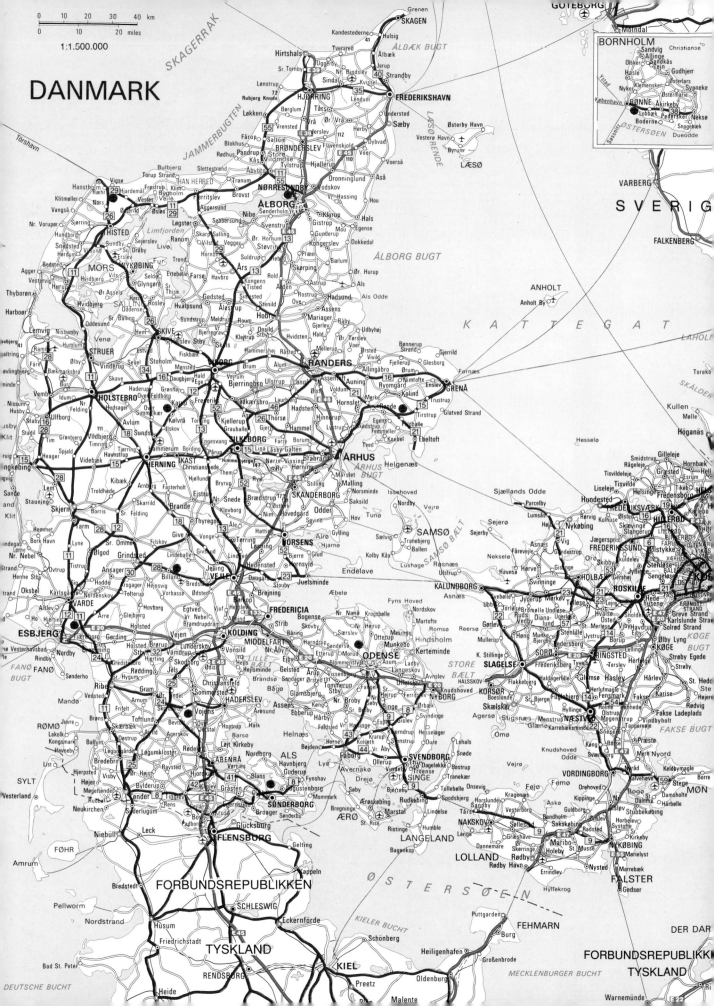

Welcome to Denmark

Her Majesty Queen Margrethe II of Denmark

Foto: Rigmor Mydtskov

DENMARK - a kingdom

Denmark is one of the "Lilliput states" in Europe and does not take up much space on the map of the world. Denmark is an island kingdom and consists of about 500 large and small islands, approximately 100 of which are inhabited. Almost half of the population live on the largest island, Zealand, whereas the smallest islands are only inhabited by a lighthouse keeper. All these islands together only cover an area of 43,069 km². However, the many islands constitute a coastline of a total of 7,500 km.

The typical Danish landscape varies between soft, round hills with small forests and fertile arable land, where lakes and rivers divide the landscape on their way to the fjords and sea. Here and there small idyllic villages are scattered with thatched houses, a village pond and church. The larger towns, the market towns, lie facing the sea, with a history which for most of them began 700-1000 years ago.

Denmark is connected by a web of countless bridges, and approximately 80 ferry routes between the different parts of the country and other countries keep the Danes together all year round.

More than 1000 km of the coastline consists of large, soft sand dunes with white sandy beaches which each year attract thousands of tourists who are eager to go swimming on their holiday. The rest of the Danish coasts vary between flat bays and deep fjords covered with sandy meadows, coastal forests and charming harbours.

At two places in eastern Denmark, at Stevn's Klint and on Møn, magnificent, white chalk cliffs tower out towards the sea, but nowhere else in Denmark will you find rocky coasts than on the sunshine island of Bornholm furthest to the east in the island kingdom.

Of Denmark's 5.2 million inhabitants, 4 million live in urban areas. Approximately 1.5 million live in Copenhagen and its suburbs alone. The second largest city is Århus in Jutland with 250,000 inhabitants and Odense in the centre of Funen comes third with 175,000 inhabitants.

The largest part of Denmark consists of the peninsula Jutland, which is joined with Germany and the European continent along a 68 km long border. Repeated wars with the great southern neighbour have moved the border up and down alternately and thereby changed the size of Denmark.

The largest island is called Zealand and is located close to Sweden, only separated by the narrow stretch of water of Øresund. Here lies the capital, Copenhagen, which throughout its more than 800 years has developed into the only Danish city with over a million inhabitants. South of Zealand lie the three neighbouring islands Lolland, Falster and Møn. The second largest island, Funen, lies sandwiched between Jutland and Zealand. It is especially known for its many castles and manors and not least for the world-famous writer of fairy-tales Hans Christian Andersen who was born and grew up in Odense. South of Funen lie a large number of islands and islets which constitute their own little island kingdom, called the Archipelago of South Funen. Here lies among others the town Ærøskøbing, which could easily be called the most charming town of Denmark with its unique 18th century houses.

All by itself, 150 km east of the rest of Denmark, lies the rocky island of Bornholm in the Baltic Sea right in the middle between Sweden and Poland. Holiday-spirited Danes like calling the island the Pearl of the Baltic Sea because of its beautiful and remarkable nature. A speciality of Bornholm is the four round churches, which were erected back in the 12th century as a mixture between churches and fortifications.

The distances in Denmark are very small. From Skagen in the north to Gedser in the south there is a mere 360 km, and from Blåvandshuk in the west to Christiansø on Bornholm in the east 450 km. No place in Denmark is further away from the sea than 50 km.

The Faroes and Greenland also belong to the Kingdom of Denmark. Both have their own parliament to take care of local matters such as school and health authorities, welfare, taxes, the environment and a number of commercial matters. They also have their own flags, languages and currencies.

The Faroes are, like Denmark, an island kingdom, which consists of 18 inhabited islands and some skerries. The islands lie together within 100 km far out in the Atlantic Ocean between Scotland and Iceland. Out there the weather is extremely unpredictable. One moment the sun is shining and it is warm, but a few minutes later the fog rolls in from the sea and covers everything on its way. The steep rocky islands provide only few possibilities for farming, so most Faroese people earn their living by means of fishing or sheep-farming. The islands have been Danish since 1380 and are sparsely inhabited by a people who have had to live and die with the sea and its vagaries as their closest neighbour.

Further to the north, all the way up under the roof of the world lies Greenland, the largest island in the world. The southern tip lies approximately at the same latitude as Oslo, whereas the northern tip, almost 3,000 km further to the north, becomes one with the ice-cap of the North Pole. Almost 90 per cent of Greenland is covered by a layer of ice which is 2 km in thickness.

The summer temperature only exceed the freezing point along the coast, and this is where the population mainly lives, on the south-west coast between cliffs and pastures. In spite of the fact that Greenland is 50 times larger than Denmark, only approximately 40,000 people live here. The original population of Greenland, the Eskimos, immigrated from Siberia and North America 700 years ago. The population has gradually mixed with European whalers and settlers, but they still have their pride as fishers, sealers and whalers, who live from nature's goods.

So if you choose to look at the Kingdom of Denmark

as including the Faroes and Greenland, it is no longer a "Lilliput State", but one of the world's "heavyweights".

The Danes' favourite topic for discussion has always been the weather, which changes from one day to the other all year round. With the sea as neighbour, the coastal climate dominates both in summer and winter. The prevailing western winds send mild and damp air from the Atlantic ocean in across the island kingdom.

The typical Danish summer alternates between lovely sunshine and periods with showers and rain. The temperature is typically 18-25°C in the daytime, but now and again there are heat waves with temperatures up to 30°C or more when the wind shifts to come from the east.

Throughout winter the temperature normally lies close to the freezing point, and it may snow one day and then rain the next. Often it is overcast and windy for long periods, and the sun hides behind the clouds for days on the shortest days in December and January.

Now and again there are, however, hard winters with severe frost and cold easterly winds from Russia. After a couple of weeks with temperatures as low as -20°C the Danish waters freeze up with close pack ice for several months, and suddenly most islands become connected with the mainland.

In May the forests burst into leaf again and Denmark shows its mild nature with many hours of sunshine and green fields.

The oldest traces of human beings in Denmark date back to the second last Ice Age approximately 240,000 years ago, but the first real culture began approximately 10,000 years BC, when the last Ice Age was on the decline. Finds of axes, spearheads and other stone tools tell about a life as fishermen, gatherers and hunters.

Around 2,500 BC some of the primeval forest which once covered the entire country was felled, and the first farms appeared with animals such as cattle, sheep, goats and pigs.

Later the Bronze Age followed in 1,800 BC, when bronze was discovered as the first metal. Numerous finds from excavations in barrows bear witness of a golden age, where weapons and beautiful ornaments were made with the finest craftsmanship. The most famous find is the unique Sun Disc with Horse, (Solvognen), which was created as a holy sculpture illustrating the sun drawn by a horse. Many thousands of barrows have been preserved as relics of the Bronze Age, scattered as small hilltops throughout the country.

As iron was discovered for production of weapons the interest in the beautiful bronze ornaments gradually declined, and in 500 BC the Iron Age began. The first real villages appeared and the houses became more solid with indoor fireplaces and thicker roofs made of grass and peat as a result of a change in the climate. New domestic animals such as chickens, dogs and cats entered. The importance of agriculture increased, because it now became possible to make better ploughs and harvest tools.

From the birth of Christ and onwards an increasing urge to explore and conquer foreign land appeared, and the period 800-1000 AD, called the Viking Age, still stands as a notorious and legendary age. Extensive plundering expeditions were organised along the coasts of Europe, and at one time the Vikings conquered England, Ireland, Normandy in Northern France, Norway and Sweden.

During a plundering expedition to Estonia in 1219 Denmark got its red and white flag, Dannebrog, which according to the legend fell down from the sky in the middle of the battle against the Estonians.

Denmark is a kingdom, in fact the oldest kingdom in the world. For 1100 years the Kingdom of Denmark has been governed by 54 monarchs counted from Gorm the Old, who died around 940. He is considered to be the first king who with certainty ruled the entire country. On the famous Jelling Stones in Jutland it is written in runes by his son, Harald Blue-Tooth, that it was Gorm the Old who unified Denmark and made the Danes Christian.

In the period until the 14th century the Royal power gradually became weaker, and the culmination of the decline of the country took place after the death of Christopher II in 1332, when the Danish kingdom fell apart. Soon better times came along, and under Margaret I the Danish kingdom was again a great power. In 1397 she was able to crown Erik of Pomerania king of Denmark, Norway and Sweden.

Sweden was lost again during the Massacre of Stockholm in 1520, whereas Norway did not become independent until 1814 as a result of the national bankruptcy of Denmark in 1813.

One of the most powerful kings, Christian IV, ruled between 1588 and 1648. He is especially known for his beautiful buildings, which can be seen today all over Copenhagen. The best knows buildings are probably the Stock Exchange building (Børsen), the Round Tower (Rundetårn), Rosenborg Castle (Rosenborg Slot) and north of Copenhagen Frederiksborg Castle (Frederiksborg Slot). Christian IV tried in vain to recapture Sweden, but after the Thirty Years' War which ended in 1660, it was instead Sweden which established itself as the great power of the Baltic Sea. The previous year the Swedish Karl X Gustav came close to occupying Denmark and great fortunes and precious furnishings from castles and manors disappeared out of the country.

From the period 1750-1807 Denmark chose a policy of neutrality during which the country recovered. Copenhagen was a great centre for trade, and trade with the Danish colonies in the Caribbean and West Africa flourished.

In 1807 the economic turning point was reached. Increasing unrest in Europe forced Denmark to join Napoleon in the war against England, who consequently bombarded Copenhagen and sunk the navy. Recession in the farming industry and increasing military costs caused inflation to rise. Six years later Denmark went bankrupt and Norway became independent the following year. Hamburg took over the economic leadership after the fall of Copenhagen, and the city was not completely rebuilt until around 1840.

In 1848 Denmark encountered new problems, as disputes about the frontier with the neighbouring country Germany about the northern Land Schleswig-Holstein resulted in the Three Years War between Denmark and Prussia. After a Danish victory in 1850 at the Battle of Isted Hede the balance of power was unchanged. Later in 1864 there was trouble again. Denmark lost not only Schleswig-Holstein, but also Southern Jutland up to the river Kongeåen. Southern Jutland was not reunited with the rest of Denmark until after World War I in 1920 after a peaceful vote. After this the Danish borders have remained unchanged until today, but in 1917 the last colonies were sold to the USA, i.e. the three small islands St. Thomas, St. Croix and St. John.

Iceland which was a part of the Danish kingdom like the Faroes and Greenland, became independent in 1944 according to its wishes.

On 9th April 1940 Hitler's Nazi troops invaded Denmark, and the country remained occupied until 5th May 1945. A wise policy of neutrality spared Denmark in the beginning as opposed to other countries, but in 1943 the situation became critical. The German military arrested the police and took over the government. Increasing sabotage and persecution of the Jews increased the unrest, and 6-7,000 Jews escaped to Sweden which was neutral and a great support until the liberation. At the end of the war 18,000 Danish refugees were staying in Sweden, but before that 2,000 policemen together with people of the Resistance and other "undesirable" people had been captured and sent to the notorious concentration camps.

Relatively few buildings were lost compared with Central Europe. The damage was greater to Danish ships, which were sunk in great numbers. A total of 136 of 230 were lost, and 950 of 7,000 seamen never returned.

After the war Denmark soon became a member of the UN and NATO, and in 1973 the Danes voted to join the Common Market, now the EU.

Queen Margaret II is now the queen of Denmark as the latest sovereign among Denmark's 54 monarchs since approximately 900 AD.

COPENHAGEN

The only big city in Denmark, Copenhagen, is situated on the eastern coast of Zealand towards Øresund with a view of Sweden. About one third, approximately one and a half million inhabitants, of Denmark's 5.2 million live here, and this makes Copenhagen the largest city of Northern Europe.

The first traces of the city date back as far as around 1000 AD, i.e. a wooden church close to the present city hall square. But Copenhagen was not really founded until 1167, when Bishop Absalon built a fortress at the original fishing hamlet. The strategically important location by the narrow stretch of water soon made the city grow, and in the 15th century it became the largest city of the country with the status of capital and both cultural and commercial dominance in the Nordic area.

Under the famous Christian IV, who governed between 1588 and 1648, a number of beautiful buildings were erected. The best known buildings are Rosenborg Castle (Rosenborg Slot), the Stock Exchange (Børsen) and the Round Tower (Rundetårn), which with their special features contribute to giving Copenhagen its character of a capital.

Numerous fires throughout the ages were unfortunately disastrous for the old market town environment. In 1728 a great fire destroyed no less than 1640 buildings, including five churches, the city hall and the university. Many of the buildings were rebuilt, but in 1794 a new fire broke out and among other places it affected the former royal palace Christiansborg. The following year a fourth of Copenhagen, approximately 950 houses, burnt down and during the English bombardments of Copenhagen in 1801 and 1807 many more old houses disappeared.

From the 1850s the city grew beyond the original ramparts, and working class quarters such as Vesterbro, Nørrebro and Østerbro appeared.

In spite of the many fires, Copenhagen can today display about 700 listed buildings, many of which are situated in beautiful location at the old ramparts around the government building Christiansborg and in Christianshavn. It is deep in here in the old Copenhagen that we find the majority of the city's sights, and there are plenty of them.

THE CITY HALL SQUARE

From of old the City Hall Square (Rådhuspladsen) has been the centre of Copenhagen. The road network extends from this square towards the south, west and north and on the stone post it says 0 km, as all distances are measured from here. Throughout this century the City Hall Square has been of great national importance, as it is tradition for people to gather by the thousands at special occasions, for instance for sports events and demonstrations. Twice the City Hall Square has held over 100,000 people, when Denmark was liberated in May 1945, and when the national football team won the European championship in the summer of 1992.

The Copenhagen City Hall is among the largest buildings in the centre, and with its location it contributes to establishing the centre of Copenhagen. The present City Hall is from 1903 and it is no less than number six in a line after the many fires. The architect Martin Nyrop was quite free to create this impressive, great building in a combination of older Danish architecture and north Italian renaissance. The actual hall of the City Hall measures approximately 1500 m² and is mainly used for weddings and official receptions. A climb up the 110 m high tower gives the visitor a sumptuous view of the red roofs of Copenhagen. Close to the main entrance you can see the famous Jens Olsen's World Clock. It has 13 synchronised works, which show the time all over the world and a number of astronomical times.

From the City Hall Square Copenhagen's two-kilometre long shopping street, Strøget, stretches down to Kongens Nytorv.

TIVOLI

Among the greatest tourist attractions of Copenhagen is the world-famous amusement park Tivoli. The original garden was founded back in 1843 by Georg Carstensen, but over the years the garden has changed its appearance many times. The two oldest buildings in the garden, the main entrance building and the Pantomime Theatre respectively, are from 1874. Only the lake is a relic from the beginning. It dates back to the original ramparts surrounding the city.

Tivoli is a festive and cultural meeting place both for Danes and foreigners offering an abundance of restaurants, amusements and entertainment for both children and adults. Scattered all over the garden you will encounter a colourful blanket of the season's flowers, which in combination with the many different fountains form a beautiful whole. Tivoli is especially romantic in the evening, when thousands of coloured lamps light the pretty Chinese buildings, and are reflected in the smooth surface of the lake with their exceptional play of colours. At various places in the garden there are countless events such as concerts, revues, plays and circus performances from the many venues. Tivoli has its own Life Guards consisting of more than 100 young people between 9 and 16 years of age. They march around the garden with brass music and festive spirits and finish with a thunder of guns to be heard all over the garden. A real evening in Tivoli ends with the spectacular fireworks, which light up the entire garden and the immediate parts of the city surrounding at midnight.

AMALIENBORG

Originally a small garden castle which was built by King Frederik III's queen Amalie was situated here. It burned down tragically in 1689, and 180 people who had gathered for a theatrical performance died. In the 1750s the present Amalienborg Palace was built in rococo style according to French design with four identical palace buildings with wings. In the beginning the palace was used as noblemen's homes, but when the original royal palace Christiansborg Palace burned down in 1794, the royal family decided to move into Amalienborg, and today Queen Margaret and Prince Henrik live in the palace building facing south-east, called Christian IX's palace. Every day the Royal Life Guard marches to music from Rosenborg and performs the Changing of the Guards at the Amalienborg Palace Square at noon, except for when the royal family is away. Then only 12-15 men march without music. On particularly festive occasions the Changing of the Life Guard takes place in the red full dress uniform, and on the queen's birthday on 16th April children and adults gather by the thousand on the Amalienborg Palace Square to cheer the queen with flags when she appears on the balcony together with the princes. In the centre of the Amalienborg Palace Square stands the equestrian statue of King Frederik V, which is considered to be one of the finest equestrian statues in the world. It took 18 years before the masterpiece by the French sculptor J.F.J. Sally could be unveiled on the palace square in 1771. Immediately behind the palace lies the new garden, Amaliehave, from 1983 which was designed by the Belgian architect Jean Delogne.

ROSENBORG PALACE

The country seat Rosenborg is definitely one of the pearls of Copenhagen. The palace was built by the renowned Christian IV in the beginning of the 17th century and was finally finished in 1634, as we know it today. Originally the king lived at Christiansborg Palace, but he gradually developed a special preference for Rosenborg, where he spent more and more time. The palace has been beautifully decorated and subsequent descendants have refined the rooms further with Italian and Chinese inspired decorations. After Frederiksberg Palace was erected in 1710, Rosenborg Palace became less attractive for the royal family, and instead the palace was used as a storage place for the personal treasures of the royal family, not least the precious regalia. The last king to live at Rosenborg Palace was Christian VII, who moved there during the English attack on Copenhagen in 1801. As of 1833 Rosenborg opened as a museum, and the precious collections have been extended over the years.

The palace offers many beautiful attractions. In addition to the treasury with the crown jewels and other jewels which are kept safely in the cellar, there is a banqueting hall with the ivory throne which through generations has been used for coronations. Several rooms are unusually pompous with stucco ceilings, tapestries, baroque decorations and precious furniture, which bear witness of a time where artistic taste and craftsmanship existed on an unsurpassed level.

The lovely park where thousands of flowers embellish the many herbaceous borders from early spring also belongs to Rosenborg.

ROUND TOWER

Another of Christian IV's great achievements is the peculiar Round Tower (Rundetårn) from 1642. Instead of a staircase there is a 209-metre long spiral ramp up through the 35-metre high tower to a gallery with a beautiful view of the roofs and spires of Copenhagen.

From the beginning it was the king's idea to build a special tower for the Trinitatis Church which is built together with the round tower, not as a bell tower but as a tower for astronomical observations, and on clear nights the public has access to the large telescope.

In 1716, during an imperial visit, the Russian empress Catherine managed to ride up the narrow spiral ramp in a horse-drawn carriage with Peter the Great in front on the horse, a feat only few have attempted!

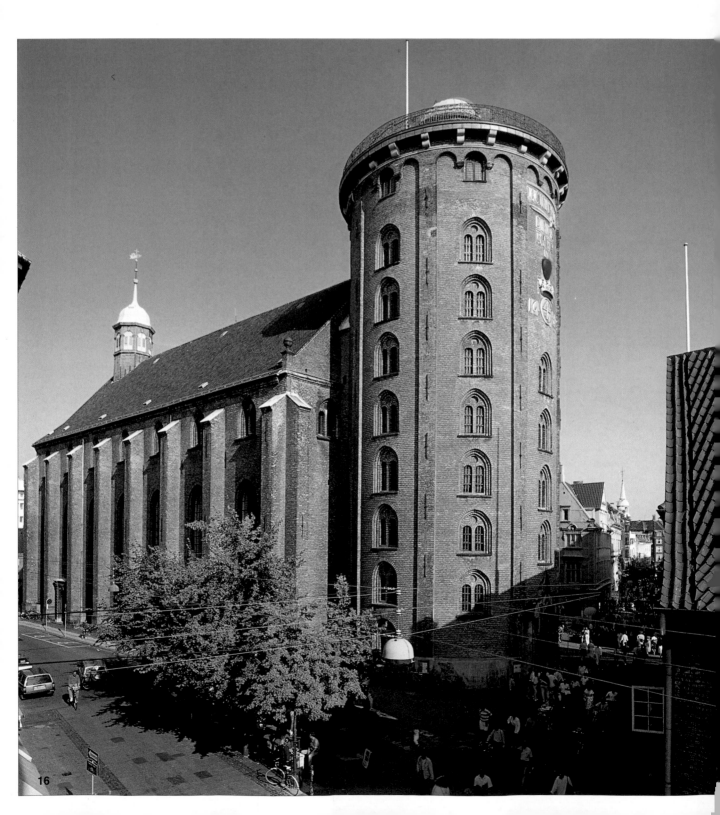

TRINITATIS CHURCH

From the Round Tower you can look through a window into Trinitatis Church which was designed by the same architect who designed the Round Tower, Hans van Steenwinckel the Younger, according to the king's idea. The foundation stone was laid on Trinity Sunday on 7th July 1637, and the church was consecrated on Trinity Sunday on 1st June 1656. The fire of Copenhagen in 1728 destroyed large parts of the church, and a new church was consecrated in 1731.

Up until 1861 the church loft held the library of Copenhagen University and irreplaceable works were lost in the fire. Today there are changing exhibitions. The famous German general Hans Schack is buried under the church. He made his career during the Thirty Years War where, among other things, he defeated the Swedish army at Nyborg. After this Schackenborg Palace was bestowed on him and he became a Danish nobleman. In 1978 Schackenborg was handed over to the royal family, and today Princess Alexandra and Prince Joachim live in the palace.

BØRSEN

The Stock Exchange, Børsen, is often regarded as one of the most remarkable buildings in Copenhagen. Again Christian IV is the originator and was behind the erection of this beautiful renaissance building with Hans v. Steenwinckel the Younger as the architect. In 1625 the 127-metre long building in two floors was ready. On the lower floor there were storage rooms for the merchants of the town, and on the first floor 36 stalls. On the outside Børsen is beautifully decorated with tortuous twigs and sandstone ornaments, which were restored most recently in 1906. Most famous is, however, the curious spire, which is made of four twisted dragon tails entirely according to the king's idea.

In 1745 a thorough restoration was carried out under the guidance of the architect Nicolai Eigtved, and the two statues of Mercury and Neptune were erected. From 1857 the large exchange hall was furnished and up until 1974 Børsen would function as the Copenhagen Stock Exchange, which at that time was the world's oldest stock exchange building still in use.

CHRISTIANSBORG PALACE

One of the largest palaces in Denmark, Christiansborg, is situated next to the Stock Exchange (Børsen). In this very place the history of Copenhagen begins. Below the palace there is an exhibition which shows remnants of the walls from the castle, which the founder of Copenhagen, Absalon, built in 1167. The castle was torn down in 1369 after the siege in 1251. Soon a new royal castle was built under Erik of Pomerania and it lasted until 1731, when, after several extensions, it had become out of date and was torn down. A beautiful palace influenced by French rococo and Viennese baroque became the royal palace in 1741. The name became Christiansborg after the reigning king Christian VI. In 1794 this magnificent palace burned to the ground. Only the riding grounds with the two rococo pavilions escaped the flames. Under Christian VII a new Christiansborg Palace was erected, but a new disastrous fire broke out in 1884 when again only the riding grounds and the chapel of the palace survived. Finally in 1916 the Christiansborg Palace which we know today was inaugurated. It was solidly faced with 7,000 granite ashlars from stones gathered in fields all over the country. Above the windows on the ground floor there are heads of famous Danish personalities carved in granite from Bornholm.

Since 1918 Christiansborg has been the home of the Danish government, the Folketing, to which there is public access. At Christiansborg you will also find the old Landsting hall, which is used today by the government and the royal family for presentations.

Behind the palace are two long buildings which are almost unchanged from the time of Christian IV. In one you will find the Royal Arsenal Museum (Tøjhusmuseet) with its unique collections of weapons and uniforms. The other one is called Proviantgården (victualling yard) and houses, among others, the National Survey and Cadastre (Kort- og Matrikelstyrelsen).

HOLMEN'S CHURCH

Another of the churches on which Christian IV has left his mark is situated by Holmen's Canal (Holmens Kanal). Originally it was an anchor smithy erected by Frederik II back in 1563, but it was fitted as a church for the fleet by his son Christian IV in 1619. Already in 1643 the church was extended by two transepts, and the neighbouring building from the 16th century was added. In 1708 the 59-metre long sepulchral chapel by the canal was built, where among others Tordenskjold, Niels Juel and Niels W. Gade are buried in beautiful sarcophagi. Out in front in the little yard a statue of the Danish naval hero Tordenskjold was also erected in 1868.

The church is richly decorated with fine wood carvings on the pulpit and altarpiece by Abel Schrøder, and on the chancel rail stand the four prophets made in the most beautiful baroque style. In addition the church is richly decorated with fine paintings by, among others, Karel van Mander and Abraham Wuchters.

NYHAVN

As is the case with Holmen's Canal, the canal along Nyhavn is also a manmade canal which was finished in 1671. The purpose was to strengthen the commercial life in the heart of Copenhagen and ease the merchant fleet's transport of goods from near and far. It was now possible to sail all the way into Kongens Nytorv and soon commercial life flourished along the new dock. Picturesque townsmen's houses appeared, and today the unique environment along the north side of Nyhavn is still preserved. The 250 year-old houses in red, yellow and blue colours are reflected in the water and constitute a beautiful interplay with the old wooden ships along the dock.

Over the years the quarter has been notorious for fights and drunken sailors, but in only a few years Nyhavn has changed into being a modern place to go out for a meal with fine pavement restaurants and expensive hotels. Today some of the ships have been converted into restaurants, houseboats and a boat theatre.

Charlottenborg Palace, which was built between 1672 and 1677, is situated on the corner of Nyhavn and Kongens Nytorv. Christian V's Queen Charlotte Amalie received the palace in 1700, hence the name. Parts of the palace are built of stones from the demolished Kalø Palace on Djursland.

Since 1753 Charlottenborg has housed the Royal Academy of Fine Arts (Det kongelige Kunstakademi) and includes schools for painters, sculptors, architects, etc., and changing exhibitions by recognised artists.

THE ROYAL THEATRE

The Royal Theatre, which was founded back in 1748 by Frederik V, is a neighbour of Charlottenborg at Kongens Nytorv. The present theatre was built between 1872 and 1874 by V. Dallerup and Ove Petersen in a kind of Italian renaissance style. The interior of the theatre is exceptionally beautiful with fine wood carvings, paintings and sculptures. At the entrance stand two statues of Adam Oehlenschläger and Ludvig Holberg respectively.

FREDERIK'S CHURCH

Originally Frederik's Church was meant to be built in connection with the erection of Amalienborg during the project which Frederik V named the Frederiksstad. The work was initiated in 1749 by the architect Nicolai Eigtved, but after his death in 1754 the new architect Jardin changed the plans in favour of a more expensive classicistic church. In 1770 the building process stopped at a height of 10 metres, as it was decided not to spend more money on the Norwegian marble, and for over 100 years the church stood as a temple ruin and thereby got the nickname the Marble Church (Marmorkirken).

Finally the ruin was bought by the financier C.F. Tietgen and the building proceeded with cheaper materials under guidance from the architect F. Meldahl, and in 1894 the church was consecrated as the largest central church in the Nordic countries. The church is exceptional and the only one in the country of its kind, which bears resemblance to a round church. When you step into the church you will be amazed at the large interior with a dome that measures 30 metres in width, and on which the 12 Apostles have been painted. A remarkable characteristic of the dome is the so-called "whispering gallery", which is created when you stand in the gallery in the dome, where sounds amplified because of the arch of the vaulted roof.

NY CARLSBERG GLYPTOTEK

As the neighbour of Tivoli lies one of Copenhagen's finest and internationally most famous museums, Ny Carlsberg Glyptotek. It was founded in 1888 by the great art collector Carl Jacobsen, who was also the man behind the Carlsberg breweries. His great interest was Danish and French contemporary art and ancient art from the cultures in the Mediterranean area. There is therefore a fine collection of paintings especially by French impressionists such as Monet, Renoir, Cézanne and Degas and younger painters such as van Gogh, Gauguin and Toulouse-Lautrec.

The collection of ancient art is quite remarkable with the original sculptures from Egypt, Italy, Greece and the Near East.

The centre of the museum is a garden with tall palm trees and subtropical plants which together with roman sarcophagi and contemporary Danish art create a peaceful harmony.

The architecture of the museum is an experience in itself. You soon notice the correlation between the lines of the building and the various works of art, entirely in the spirit of Carl Jacobsen.

Already in 1902 the foundation Ny Carlsbergfondet was set up to ensure the running of the museum and thanks to those funds the collections are supplemented on a continuous basis with new valuable objects of art.

THORVALDSEN'S MUSEUM

By Holmen's Canal next to Christiansborg lies a beautiful yellow building in the finest neo-classicistic style, created by M.G. Bindesbøll. This building houses Thorvaldsen's Museum in memory of the great Danish sculptor and painter Bertel Thorvaldsen (1770-1844). On the outside the museum has been decorated with a frieze showing Thorvaldsen's homecoming from Rome in 1838. Inside there are also numerous decorations which create a harmonic balance with Thorvaldsen's marble sculptures.

The museum mainly contains his numerous sculptures which were inspired by Antiquity. A simple and calm beauty characterises Thorvaldsen's art, where peacefulness and harmony are the focus. The artist made a large number of statues in Rome, which made him known abroad. Upon his return Thorvaldsen donated his works and fine art collections and his entire fortune to the establishment of a museum. It took almost ten years to build the museum which Thorvaldsen never saw completed before his death in 1844. Four years later he was buried in the courtyard of the museum.

THE DANISH NATIONAL GALLERY

The same architect, V. Dahlerup, who built the Ny Carlsberg Glyptotek, was assigned the task of building a museum for the art collection of the royal family, and in 1896 the museum was ready to be inaugurated in beautiful Italian renaissance forms. It is Denmark's largest museum with the most important art collection of Scandinavia. Inside the museum can be divided into two main sections. There is a large collection of Danish paintings which date back to the 17th century, and a number of sculptures which have been placed beautifully among each other. The many paintings from the Danish "Golden Age" by artists such as Skovgaard, Lundbye, Eckersberg and Købke dominate. There are also significant collections of mainly older Italian, French and Dutch paintings by, among others, Rembrandt and Matisse. Furthermore, there is a special French modern art collection, the famous Rump Collection, which was donated by the engineer J. Rump in 1928. The museum's royal collection of prints by Eckersberg and Goya is quite unique.

THE BOTANICAL GARDENS

The Botanical Gardens (Botanisk Have) lie in the centre of Copenhagen as a breathing hole opposite the Danish National Gallery. They were landscaped between 1871 and 74 on parts of the old ramparts which surrounded Copenhagen. The idea behind the gardens was to donate a garden for studies to the students of the university with various herbs, bushes and trees from all parts of the world. In the centre of the gardens lies the Palm House (Palmehuset), a greenhouse with tropical plants, which constitute a small jungle. Via a winding staircase you can get high up and view the plants from above.

All around the park paths have been laid out for walking, and a couple of lakes have also been laid out with an overgrown wooden bridge.

TYCHO BRAHE PLANETARIUM

The quite unique design of the Planetarium building is among the most remarkable sights in Copenhagen. In the Planetarium it is possible to render the starry sky just as it looks on a clear night by means of modern computer technology. The domed screen has a diameter of 23 metres and the sound reproduction is very advanced with special effects. On the hour films are shown which have been recorded and reproduced in such a remarkable way that the effects from the movements in the film make the experience extremely real, and the audience will feel as though they are there themselves.

← *Botanisk Have*

THE GEFION FOUNTAIN

On the way towards Langelinje slightly north of the centre you will find the largest fountain in Copenhagen, the Gefion Fountain (Gefionspringvandet) which was made by Anders Bundgaard in 1908. The fountain shows the ploughing scene from an old legend in Nordic mythology. According to the legend the Nordic goddess of fertility, Gefion, was promised as much land by the Swedish King Gylfe as she was able to plough in 24 hours. Gefion then turned her four sons into oxen and ploughed Zealand out of Sweden where the lake Mälaren is situated today west of Stockholm.

LANGELINJE

On the Langelinje dock at the entrance to Copenhagen sits what is probably the best known statue in Denmark, The Little Mermaid (Den lille Havfrue). It was made in bronze by the sculptor Edvard Eriksen in 1913 as a memory of the fairy-tale The Little Mermaid by Hans Christian Andersen. The statue has become world famous and stands as a symbol of Copenhagen and Denmark.

THE NATIONAL MUSEUM

The National Museum (Nationalmuseet) is situated in the large rococo building called the Prince's Palace (Prinsens Palæ) between Christiansborg Castle and Tivoli Gardens. It is nothing less than Denmark's oldest rococo palace in pure French design built by the famous engineer N. Eigtved in 1744 as a home for crown prince Frederik V. From the middle of the 19th century various museum pieces were collected and this collection developed into the creation of the Danish National Museum in 1892.

Today the National Museum is the largest museum of cultural history in the country, and it contains endless collections of ancient items from prehistoric times and onwards. Among the most famous finds are the Sun Disc with Horse (Solvognen), the Lures (Lurerne) and the Gold Horns (Guldhornene).

The museum holds many other collections such as the Antique Collection, the Ethnographic Collection, the Coin Collection, the Natural Science Section and the Victorian Home.

Solvognen

THE OPEN-AIR MUSEUM

In Lyngby north of Copenhagen you will find the popular Open-air Museum (Frilandsmuseet), which belongs under the National Museum. Here you will find a wide selection of old farms, country houses, wind and water mills scattered in the large park with domestic cats and flocks of tame geese walking about freely. All the farms are richly equipped with furniture and domestic equipment which is typical for the time and place, showing how Danes lived in the old days. The many different buildings have been carefully taken apart and collected from all parts of Denmark and then rebuilt unchanged brick by brick. Here and there you will find workshops for historical craft demonstrations of pottery, weaving and lace-making. At the end you can take a tour around the museum in a horse-drawn carriage.

JÆGERSBORG DEER PARK

Along the coast of Øresund north of Copenhagen lies the Deer Park (Dyrehaven), a very old forest which Frederik III fenced in in 1669 for the royal hunts. Today the forest is dominated by beeches, but here and there you will still find the large, crooked oaks which are many centuries old. The forest has a large deer population of 2,000 fallow deer, 300 royal stags and some sika deer, but no roe deer.

A lovely country seat is situated in the centre of the forest on the Hermitage Plain (Eremitagesletten) in a beautiful location between barrows, oaks and herds of deer. It is the Hermitage Palace which Christian VI built between 1734 and 36 as a hunting seat in a Saxon rococo style. The palace is still used in connection with the royal hunts in the autumn.

From old times the Deer Park has been a place for entertainment. Already from 1585 people came to visit the curative spring, Kirsten Piils Kilde, and soon a tradition for performers and other types of entertainment developed here. Throughout the last hundred years the entertainment has developed into roller-coasters, merry-go-rounds, shooting booths, all sorts of stalls and public houses. The place is called Bakken and nowadays it is a popular excursion spot for Copenhageners in the summer.

DRAGØR

South of Copenhagen and Kastrup Airport lies the fishing town Dragør, which with its yellow, well-preserved half-timbered houses and narrow cobbled streets is one of the most charming ports in Denmark. The old part of the town has practically been left unchanged throughout the last centuries, but Dragør already came into being in the Middle Ages and was of great importance to herring fishing in Øresund. The town grew quickly from the 1520s when Christian II brought a group of Dutchmen to Amager to cultivate and preserve the fertile land.

At Dragør Museum, situated in the oldest house in the town, you can see part of the town's history with focus on collections from the sailing-ship period and the old traditional costumes of Dragør. Close by you will find a small museum for the Dragør painter Christian Mølsted, where you can experience his many paintings from the turn of the century.

THE KAREN BLIXEN MUSEUM

Rungstedlund, which has been the museum of the world-famous Danish writer and poet Karen Blixen since 1991 is situated on the shore of Øresund right between Copenhagen and Elsinore. She began her career in America, but soon her fame would reach most of the world. Karen Blixen spent most of her life at Rungstedlund. She was born here in 1885 and she died here in 1962. For 17 years she lived on a coffee farm in Kenya, from which some of her inspiration came. After eight years of marriage she was separated from her husband the Swedish baron Bror von Blixen-Finecke in 1921, and took over the operation of the coffee farm. The farm was later given up and she returned to Denmark in 1931 and moved in at Rungstedlund, where Karen Blixen began to write her wonderful works. Among her most famous books is beyond any doubt Out of Africa, which was the basis of a major Oscar-winning film in 1985 which was shown in cinemas all over the world.

Karen Blixen's father Wilhelm Dinesen acquired Rungstedlund, which was originally an inn, Rungsted Kro, in 1879, but the history of Rungstedlund goes back almost 500 years. The present buildings are from the beginning of the 19th century. In 1958, four years before her death, Karen Blixen set up the fund Rungstedlundfonden, which in addition to the buildings includes an area of 16 ha of land with a park and bird reserve. At the museum you can experience her home unchanged, as she originally furnished and decorated it. At the museum you will also have the opportunity to see slides from Karen Blixen's years in Africa and hear her fascinating voice.

Karen Blixen, 1913 photo: Sophus Juncker-Jensen

Karen Blixen, 1942 photo: Rie Nissen

Rungstedlund

LOUISIANA

Denmark's most famous museum of modern art Louisiana lies with a view of Øresund on the road Strandvejen towards Elsinore. It all started in a 150-year-old house in 1958, but soon large extensions were built to the museum from which there is a panoramic view of the beautiful park through the large glass fa_ades. Here you will experience the unique interplay between nature, architecture and art. Numerous sculptures by recognised artists from all over the world, such as Arp, Caldar, Ernst and Moore are scattered in the park which stretches from the lake Humlebæk Sø through small hills with old trees to the coast of Øresund.

Inside Louisiana holds changing exhibitions by artists from all over the world side by side with the permanent exhibition. Here names such as Warhol, Jorn, Vasarely, Alechinsky and Weie are represented.

FREDERIKSBORG CASTLE

Denmark's most beautiful renaissance castle, Frederiksborg Slot, is situated in the centre of North Zealand in the town Hillerød. The history of the castle dates back to Frederik II who took over the manor of Hillerødsholm in 1560 from Herluf Trolle. Shortly after began the building of a new castle, and today its towers can still be seen at the S-shaped bridge, the buildings at Sydholmen and the small country seat Badstuen (the bath).

By 1602 his son Christian IV had begun the erection of the Frederiksborg Castle which we know today. The old manor of Hillerødsholm was torn down the year before and with the income from the Øresund Duty the magnificent castle was created and inaugurated in 1625.

During the Swedish occupation between 1658 and 1660 the castle was severely damaged, and the Swedish queen Hedvig Eleonora, who lived at the castle for some time, robbed it of precious furnishings which ended up at Drottningholm Castle by Stockholm. The next king, Frederik III, had to use great sums to recreate the castle, but subsequent kings have sold part of the precious furniture because of pecuniary distress.

The great national disaster occurred on 17th December 1859, when King Frederik VII asked to have a fire started in a broken fireplace without firebricks. Soon the entire Frederiksborg Castle was ablaze, and as the castle lake was frozen, the castle could not be saved. Only the chapel of the castle and the Audience House (Audienshuset) and the Mint Gate (Møntporten) escaped the fire.

The fire disaster was regarded as a national misfortune and generated public mourning. Soon a national collection was initiated and both Iceland and Holstein participated, and not least with capital from the brewer J.C. Jacobsen, who founded Carlsberg, the castle could be inaugurated again in 1878.

Frederiksborg Castle was resurrected as a national historical museum and was opened to the public in 1885. Today it is a unique portrait gallery with both collections which were saved during the fire and countless beautiful pictures which have been collected from all over the country or painted later by the leading artists in the country. An abundance of furniture which has been carefully selected for the great rooms can also be seen. As late as 1996 a baroque garden was recreated with a fountain and the monogram of Queen Margaret II as a border.

FREDENSBORG PALACE

Another of North Zealand's three famous castles and palaces is situated only 8 km north-east of Frederiksborg Castle. Like a white pearl Fredensborg Palace raises its whitewashed walls up over the palace park right behind the town. Fredensborg is the youngest of the three constructions and was inaugurated in 1722 on Frederik IV's birthday. The name is a tribute to the peace after the Great Nordic War (Store Nordiske Krig) in 1720. Influenced by his travels in Italy, Frederik IV built the palace in Italian renaissance style, although Frederiksborg Castle, which the king found was old and out of date, was situated close by. Fredensborg Palace was mainly important as a summer residence, but after the fire disaster at Frederiksborg in 1859 it was really taken into use by Christian IX for a period. The palace was visited frequently by European kings and emperors who came to take vacations in the beautiful surroundings.

The palace is also used today by the royal family. Part of the year Fredensborg Palace is used by Queen Margaret and Prince Henrik as summer residence, but in the month of July it is open to the public and is definitely worth a visit. Inside the palace there are magnificent paintings on both walls and ceilings with motifs from the Trojan cycle of legends which were made in the period about 1760. The lavish interiors change between baroque and rococo, and you sense a little of the atmosphere from the time of the great Danish writer Ludvig Holberg.

The palace gardens are an experience in themselves. A system of paths runs from the palace at angles of 30° in the shape of a half star, which once was the setting for the hunting paths of the forest. The fragrance from flowering bushes and perennials is noticeable all over the gardens, which stretch all the way down to the lake Esrum Sø. A marble garden with sculptures by the sculptors Krieger and Wiedewelt was landscaped according to French style. On the island in the octagonal lake Pagodesøen an aviary was placed, where the visitors at the palace could look at singing tropical birds. Further down in the park there is the exciting and unique sculpture park Normandsdalen with 69 sandstone figures of Norwegian fishermen and peasants carved by J.G. Grundt.

ELSINORE (HELSINGØR)

The history of Elsinore goes back to 1231, when Valdemar Sejr mentions the town as the market town Ørekrog, but the beach probably served as a fishing hamlet and ferry berth long before the Middle Ages. In around 1429 Erik of Pomerania introduced the Øresund Toll which forced all passing foreign commercial ships to pay a duty to the Danish king in this bottleneck between Denmark and Sweden, and this was later to become very profitable. While the ships were at anchor the crew were free to do business with merchants and craftsmen, and then later enjoy the town's night life. The toll was not abolished until 1857 under Frederik VII, but at that time the town had prospered from 428 years' earnings from the ship traffic.

Today Elsinore is a lively port with a frequent ferry service to Helsingborg every 15 minutes. In spite of several fires a veritable treasure of beautiful, protected houses has been preserved from the golden age of Elsinore. Oxe's Gaard from the 1480s and Apotekhuset from approximately 1520, both in a gothic style, face the small passage, Gl. Færgestræde, which only measures 2.3 metres across.

On the edge of the town lies the small renaissance country seat Marienlyst Palace which was created by the French architect Jardin in 1763. Here and in the neighbouring Carmelite House (Karmeliterhuset) there is now a town museum.

KRONBORG CASTLE

At the entrance to Øresund only a few hundred metres from the centre of Elsinore towers the large renaissance castle Kronborg. From this place there are only 4 km to the coast of Skåne in Sweden, and therefore the castle was of great importance for the collection of the Øresund Toll until 1857. Originally Krogen Castle was situated here, and it was built by Erik of Pomerania shortly before the Øresund Toll was introduced. Under Frederik II Krogen Castle was completely rebuilt, and in 1585 the present Kronborg Castle was inaugurated, completely financed by earnings from the toll.

But Kronborg Castle was to share the fate of Frederiksborg Castle and other Danish castles. In 1629, during the confinement of the wife of Christian IV, Kirsten Munk, a fire broke out which only spared a few sections of the castle and the chapel. Only eight years later the castle had been rebuilt, but during the Dano-Swedish War in 1658 it suffered misfortune again. Great treasures were carried off, including the great fountain and Frederik II's beautiful canopy. Kronborg was repaired again, but gradually the castle lost its value as a royal home. Between 1758 and 1922 Kronborg only operated as a military barracks and was damaged and not maintained until museum officials started recreating the values which today constitute the basis of the largest renaissance castle of Northern Europe.

Holger Danske

The international fame of Elsinore and Kronborg is not least due to William Shakespeare's immortal play about prince Hamlet, who meets his father's ghost on the bastions of Kronborg. Today Kronborg is a museum, which offers a fine interior with the characteristics of a royal residence. The two chambers, the Queen's Chamber and the King's Chamber are richly equipped with beautiful door frames, ceiling paintings and fireplaces in marble. The banqueting hall is the largest in Europe with its length of 62 metres.

In the casemates of Kronborg you will find the most popular figure in the castle. It is the Danish national hero, Holger Danske, who has been sitting here sleeping since his great feats in the battles against Muslims and heathens in the dark Middle Ages. According to legend Holger Danske will not wake up to fight until the day Denmark is in severe danger.

The Commercial and Maritime museum is an independent section at Kronborg. Here Danish trade and shipping through the ages is described, including among others the merchant fleet, lighthouse authority, travels to China and the Danish colonies in the West Indies.

GILLELEJE

The northernmost town of Zealand, Gilleleje, has almost everything to offer the many tourists who visit the holiday town every year. West of the port the cliff Gilbjerg Hoved rises 33 metres over the sea, and in spring, when the wind comes from the south-east, you can see large flights of birds migrating north towards Kullen, which can be distinguished when the weather is clear. Along the path to Gilbjerg Hoved you will find the monument to the Danish philosopher Søren Kirkegaard.

The many old fisherman's cottages which grace the town of Gilleleje bear witness of proud traditions as a fishing society. A museum in the former school from 1897 describes the cultural lives of the coastal peasants and fishermen from prehistoric times until the 19th century. Here are shown old fishing equipment, old traditional costumes and a fine collection of archaeological finds. The old house on the main street Hovedgaden 49 has been made up as a 19th century fisherman's home. Today Gilleleje has the largest fishing port on Zealand with approximately 40 cutters and many smaller boats which land fish of a value of approximately DKK 50 million each year, including herring, cod and virgin lobster.

The lighthouse Nakkehoved Fyr is situated just east of Gilleleje on top of the steep slopes to the beach. With a height of the light of 54 metres, the cone of light today reaches over 40 km out over the Kattegat and has guided the ship traffic for 200 years. In the hinterland there are many protected barrows. Maglehøje south-west of Udsholt consists of eight large fine barrows from the farming Stone Age and Bronze Age.

ROSKILDE CATHEDRAL

The most distinguished church of Denmark, Roskilde Cathedral (Roskilde Domkirke) is situated no more than 30 km west of Copenhagen. Raised high over one of the oldest cities in the country lies this stately church which was begun in the time of Absalon, at the same time as the foundation of Copenhagen, but has been changed much over the years. The church is very impressive with its large interior and the lavish furnishings from historic monuments and beautiful works of art to the unique sepulchral chapels. In this church 20 kings and 17 queens have been interred in addition to a large number of personalities from the nobility and clergy. Among the oldest sarcophagi is the one with Margaret I who died from the plague in 1412. Also the famous king Christian IV and his wife Queen Cathrine lie here. An amusing detail in the chapel of Christian I is the king's column which indicates the height of 24 sovereigns. First comes the Tzar Peter the Great with 208 cm, whereas Christian VII only measured 164 cm.

Originally Roskilde Cathedral had even more precious furnishings, but during an attack on the church in 1534, shortly before the Reformation, irreplaceable objects disappeared. In spite of this the church is richer and more pompous today than any other Danish church thanks to great efforts.

KALUNDBORG CHURCH

The only church in Denmark with five towers is situated by the west coast of Zealand in one of the oldest towns in the country, Kalundborg. Nowhere else will you find a church with such a special appearance. It was erected between 1170 and 1190 by Esbern Snare, a brother of Absalon, the founder of Copenhagen. The church is situated on high ground and can be seen from far away. Inside the church is surprisingly small, with a relatively modest interior, except for the large altarpiece with the finely carved wooden figures which was made by Lorentz Jørgensen in 1650. The central tower could not withstand a storm in 1827 and collapsed. The altarpiece and the pulpit were severely damaged and not until 40 years later was the present central tower resurrected.

At the same time as Kalundborg Church was erected, a stronghold was built close by. Here the Danish king Christian II was imprisoned between 1549 and 1559. During the Swedish occupation in 1658 the stronghold was attacked and levelled with the ground. Only a few remains of the walls have been preserved, and can be seen in the park of ruins.

GAVNØ MANOR

This stately manor and park is situated in South Zealand just south of Næstved. The present main building with three wings got its present appearance in 1758, when the manor was expanded by the owner Otto Thott. He was a prosperous nobleman and in time he acquired a large collection of books and an immense collection of paintings. A visit to the manor shows a rich assortment of furniture and precious porcelain in addition to the many paintings. In the beautiful banqueting hall you will see the magnificent rococo stucco ceiling and carved door frames which date back as far as the 1580s. The chapel of the manor is even older and dates back to the 15th century, when there was a convent here. In the chapel you will find, among other things, fine wood carvings preserved from the 1660s.

But what Gavnø Manor is probably best known for is the vast, impressive manor park. In the spring you will notice the scent from flowering tulips and other flowers by the thousand all over the garden. In the centre of the garden you will find a Butterfly World (Sommerfugleland) in a greenhouse with a tropical climate , where large butterflies and birds fly freely. In addition there is the Falck Museum where old fire engines are exhibited.

MØN

The island of Møn is situated in the Baltic Sea between Zealand and Falster. The 8 km long chalk cliff, Møn's Klint, which stretches from the lighthouse, Møn's Fyr, in the south to Liselund Manor in the north is magnificent. Out here the winding forest paths lead you past peaks and slopes and give you one beautiful view of the cliffs after the other. From the viewpoints you will experience the sight of the vertiginous precipice, where deep down the Baltic Sea with an exceptional interplay of colours with bluish green reflections form a sharp contrast to the light green beeches and the white chalk. The porous cliff is dangerous and you should not attempt to climb it, but follow the marked paths and steps down to the beach.

The history of the cliff goes back 75 million years. The chalk originates from fossilised shellfish, which fell down to the bottom of the sea, and the actual cliff was created during the Ice Age, where the ice cap pushed the chalk forward in its movement towards the west.

On the north cliff lies the fairy-tale manor Liselund. Inspired by Rousseau's ideas of returning to nature and living in peaceful surroundings, the French nobleman Antoine de Bosc de la Calmette landscaped this romantic park in the 1780s with dammed lakes and small country houses according to the English style. It is an impressive sight to see Liselund Manor reflect its white-washed walls in the smooth water of the lake. Although the park has been reduced significantly because of erosion, the entire park has a harmonic appearance as a relic from a time when artistic taste and craftsmanship met on an unsurpassed level.

AALHOLM

In Nysted on the island of Lolland lies one of the two main attractions of the island, Aalholm Castle with the Automobile Museum (Veteranbilmuseet). The history of the castle probably begins around the year 1300, when it was a fortress with many towers, and it was placed as an island fort on a small islet. In 1328 Aalholm appears from the darkness of history for the first time, when king Christopher II mortgaged both Lolland and Falster to his half brother in Holstein, Count Johan the Mild. Three years later the king ended up imprisoned at the castle. Under Valdemar Atterdag Denmark became one kingdom again and Aalholm was liberated in 1347. After this it remained one of the preferred places of the Crown for some part of the Middle Ages and many famous sovereigns such as Valdemar Atterdag and his daughter Margaret I, Erik of Pomerania, Christopher of Bavaria and Frederik II have stayed here. In 1726 the castle became privately owned and has remained so ever since. Aalholm has always been luxuriously furnished by the changing owners. Some of the furnishings were, however, sold in 1995. The castle's neighbour is Aalholm Motor Museum (Veteranbilmuseet) which has been fitted in the old home farm Stubberupgård. Here one of the finest collections of vintage cars in Europe has been assembled by the latest baron at the castle Johan Otto Raben-Levetzau. Many of the cars are completely intact and are in roadworthy condition.

KNUTHENBORG SAFARI PARK

Along the north side of the coast of Lolland lies nothing less than the largest privately owned park in Northern Europe measuring 660 ha, surrounded by a 7.2 km long field stone wall. Originally the park was laid out in the 1860s according to the English style in estate surroundings with a manor, home farm and park. Around the park several miniature manors were built, among others the residence of the forest supervisor (Skovridderboligen) and the flint stone house (Flintestenshuset). Around 500 different bushes and trees from near and far were planted and were an attraction in themselves, not least the large rhododendron borders. Count Knuth did not open the actual safari park until 1970, for which large numbers of animals from Africa and Asia were collected. On the savannah-like grazing grounds herds of giraffes, zebras, gnus, rhinoceroses, ostriches, deer and elephants walk around freely between the cars, which have 16 km of road to drive around on in the park. In two specially enclosed areas there are the baboon park and the tiger park, where it is strictly prohibited to get out of the car.

At the bottom of the park there is both a steam train and a funfair, where you can see a miniature version of Lolland-Falster in the scale 1:1000.

FUNEN

The beautiful, fertile island of Funen (Fyn) is situated well protected between Jutland and Zealand, which the fairy-tale writer Hans Christian Andersen rightly called "The garden of Denmark". Here the castles and manors lie closer together than at any other place in the world and more than 150 of them have been preserved mainly on South Funen. To each of these buildings belong beautiful parks, old avenues, moats with water lilies and a number of stone walls, winding their way across the vast neighbouring fields.

Along the small winding roads far off the beaten track numerous half-timbered houses in pretty red, white and yellow appear and grace the many villages all over Funen. Most of South and West Funen is characterised by a lovely hilly landscape with small forests and water mills. From the highest point on Funen, Frøbjerg Bavnehøj, 134 metres above sea level, there is a magnificent view over the entire Small Belt (Lille Bælt) and far into Southern Jutland.

Hesselagergaard

Kaleko Mølle

ODENSE

Odense is Denmark's third largest city, situated in the heart of Funen as a "capital". In 1988 the city celebrated its 1000th anniversary, but archaeological finds from the city's soil date significantly further back in time. Among the many sights Odense can offer is the Funen Village (Den fynske Landsby). Over 20 old houses and farms have been collected from all over Funen, and with its small historical workshops you can feel a little of the village atmosphere which existed at the time of Hans Christian Andersen. The old cathedral of the city, St Knud's Church (Sankt Knuds Kirke) is situated near the city hall. Here you can see the impressive altarpiece, which is a total of 5 metres high and has over 300 different wooden figures which were made around 1520 by the German Claus Berg. The earthly remains of the Danish king Knud the Holy (Knud den Hellige), who was murdered in 1086 by rebellious peasants in St. Alban's Church (Skt. Albani Kirke) in Odense are contained in one of the many sepulchral monuments for the nobility.

Most famous and of international renown is the quarter around the childhood home of Hans Christian Andersen, and tourists flock from all over the world to the famous museum for the fairy-tale writer. The poet's belongings, various manuscripts and letters, a number of illustrations for the fairy-tales and a library have been collected here. An attempt has been made to recreate his childhood home carefully with furniture and other items. The actual quarter has undergone thorough reconstruction. The cobbled streets have returned and the small, low houses have been restored, and others have been moved here. In this way an attempt has been made to revert the external environment to the time of Hans Christian Andersen in the beginning of the 19th century, but inside the popular houses have been completely modernised.

EGESKOV CASTLE

The most impressive of the manors of Funen and quite unique is Egeskov Castle (Egeskov Slot), which is considered to be among the best preserved island forts in Europe and it is said that it was built on an entire forest of oak trunks in 1554. This distinctive and decorative castle is bound to appeal to your fantasy like no other Danish manor house. A motor museum with cars, motorcycles, carriages and aeroplanes also belongs to the castle. The surrounding park is an experience in itself with many beautiful types of garden and a quite unique maze.

ÆRØ

The waters south of Funen are called the Archipelago of South Funen (Det sydfynske Øhav) which is a piece of nature with no comparison to the rest of Denmark, and each summer it becomes an eldorado for sailing tourists. The old town of Ærø, Ærøskøbing, could easily be called the most charming town of Denmark with its over 170 old, listed buildings, which have been spared the fires. Here you will find low, yellow and red half-timbered houses, narrow, twisted alleys and cobblestones. On the square the town's two old water pumps have been preserved, and they are still working. The entire town is the epitome of romance and nostalgia with its unchanged and well preserved environment. It is almost as though time has stood still since the 18th century in this corner of Denmark.

Ærøskøbing

LANGELAND

South of Funen next to Ærø a 52-km long narrow island stretches up through the Great Belt (Store Bælt). The nature of the island is somewhat different from that of the rest of the country with its hundreds of so-called drumlins, which are small, round hills with a height of between 20 and 45 metres. In some places a hill ends by the water and forms a beautiful sea cliff. This is the exact place where the Danish poet Oehlenschläger was so inspired when he saw the light green beeches reflected in the water that he wrote the Danish national anthem, "Der er et yndigt land" (there is a lovely country) almost 200 years ago. Even though the idyll of Langeland is to be found in the actual landscape with the small winding roads and hedgerows between the hills, the island has other exciting things to offer. Of the original 15 mills, most have been preserved and several beautiful manors and palaces rise up above the landscape. The best known is the red Tranekær Manor (Tranekær Slot) on the road towards the north. It has been the dominating manor of Langeland for almost 800 years. The wonderful atmosphere has been preserved when you drive along the winding road past the picturesque, yellow half-timbered houses and encounter Tranekær Manor high above the town and the lake on its mound. Another magnificent manor, Skousgaard, is situated on the southern part of the island and was built in neo-renaissance style as late as 1889. A museum with old horse-drawn carriages, hansoms, etc. has been installed in the stables belonging to the manor

Tranekær Slot

← Skousgaard   *Lindelse Kirke*

KOLDINGHUS

The first Koldinghus was built in Kolding in Eastern Jutland when the border between the Kingdom of Denmark and Duchy of Schleswig ran here in the middle of the 13th century. Today there are no remains left from the original castle which King Erik Glipping built to protect the kingdom's border toward the south. Up through the unsettled Middle Ages, Koldinghus became of great national importance to the Danish monarchs, and under Christian I in the middle of the 15th century the main parts of the castle which exist today were built. Koldinghus was converted to a royal palace and the ramparts were removed in the 1530s under Christian III after the bloody civil war Grevens Fejde (the count's quarrel). To disguise the different building periods Koldinghus was whitewashed and the roof was covered with green slate for a long period. In 1808 a great fire disaster occurred. Denmark was at war with England, which had taken the entire Danish navy in the previous year. The Emperor Napoleon had sent 30,000 men, mainly Spanish mercenaries, to Jutland. The purpose was to secure Denmark, but also to recapture Skåne, Halland and Blekinge in southern Sweden. On 29th March a troop of Spanish soldiers were accommodated at Koldinghus, and the Spaniards, who were very sensitive to the cold, built up such a large fire that a defective chimney caught fire. In two days Koldinghus was transformed to a smoking ruin. Unfortunately the treasury was empty after the wars with England, and the palace was not rebuilt, but the external parts of the old Koldinghus have been restored periodically up until today. In this way Koldinghus appears today as a mixture of ruins and reconstructed palace, and it has become an attractive museum in the area. Among the well-equipped rooms are the banqueting hall and the beautiful, white library hall. From the 41 metre high tower there is an infinite view of the town of Kolding and the fjord.

LEGOLAND

One of the greatest ever commercial successes, the toy factory Lego, is situated in the centre of Jutland close to Billund. Since it was established in 1932 Lego has developed into a global product with its small plastic bricks. In 1968 Legoland opened and today it is an amusement park for children and adults, and it is built from approximately 33 million Lego bricks. Many famous sights such as Amalienborg and Nyhavn in Copenhagen have been built in miniature in Lego, but also the heads of the four American presidents that are carved into Mount Rushmore, and a western town can be seen.

Another sight to be seen at Legoland is the internationally famed doll's house, Titanic Palace from 1922. Here you can see approximately 2,000 objects placed in 22 rooms. In addition there is a large number of completely irreplaceable dolls and doll's houses dating back to 1580 and onwards. All this has made Legoland the greatest tourist attraction in Jutland.

A few kilometres from Legoland lies another sight of the region, the Lion Park in Givskud. Here you will find approximately 45 species of mammals walking freely on grazing grounds in this safari land. The lions are kept safely behind a separate fence, however.

DYBBØL MILL

The famous Dybbøl Mill (Dybbøl Mølle) is situated in Southern Jutland by the island of Als close to the border with Germany as a landmark of the wars against Germany in the 19th century. With its central location on the top of the 68-metre high hill, Dybbøl Banke, the mill became a passive witness to the bloody battles. First Denmark won over Germany during the Three Years War in 1848, but in spite of redoubt constructions in the meantime, Denmark suffered a severe defeat over Southern Jutland in 1864. After this the Danish-German border was moved north to the river Kongeåen between Ribe and Kolding. Southern Jutland was not reunited with Denmark until after a peaceful vote in 1920. Dybbøl Mill has been rebuilt a total of three times after the bombardments 1848 and 1864, and after a fire in 1936.

In the centre of the redoubt area and the memorial park lies the Historical Centre Dybbøl Banke, which gives a vivid description of how the soldiers experienced the war in sound and pictures. Uniforms and weapons from that time are also exhibited. In clear weather there is a formidable view from the mill across Sønderborg and the entire beautiful Flensborg Fjord.

SØNDERBORG CASTLE

With its view of Sønderborg Bay (Sønderborg Bugt) down towards Germany this castle contains much history up through the unsettled Middle Ages. Since the 12th century the most important function of the castle has been to protect the Danish kingdom against the enemies from the south. The castle is especially known for the fact that the Danish king Christian II was imprisoned here in a tower between 1532 and 1549, and a famous painting by Carl Bloch shows a table with a groove which had appeared after the king had walked around the table restlessly with his index finger pressed down on the table. The table has never existed, and more recent investigations reveal that the king had access to the entire castle, had many servants and even a jester. After a thorough rebuilding of the castle in 1720 it got its present appearance, and after the reunification with Denmark in 1920 it was converted into a museum. Here the history of Southern Jutland can be experienced, including the castle's own old history. In addition there is a collection of paintings by local painters from Denmark's Golden Age such as C.W. Eckersberg and C.A. Lorentzen.

From olden times Southern Jutland has been known for its tilting at the ring, a competition where men on horseback with a lance must attempt to put it through a ring which is hanging in the air. This was a popular entertainment for the Court between the 16th and 18th centuries. Tilting at the ring can be experienced in various towns in Southern Jutland every summer.

TØNDER

Tønder lies in the south-western corner of Denmark. Right from 1130 Tønder was known as an active port in spite of the fact that it is situated 10 km from the sea today. After the building of dikes in the 1550s as a guard against the frequent floods caused by high winds, land was recovered and the proud seafaring traditions of Tønder disappeared. An extensive lace industry then flourished, and in the 18th century it developed into the main occupation of Tønder, employing approximately 12,000 lacemakers. Making lace became a highly regarded occupation which provided the citizens with good incomes. In that period the special, well-protected gable houses with bays appeared, so that the lacemakers got sufficient light in the rooms and so that they could also keep an eye on the street-life. The town also has a remarkable number of beautiful front doors from Tønder's golden age.

Tønder Museum and the South Jutland Art Museum (Sønderjyllands Kunstmuseum) are situated in the old gatehouse of Tønder Castle which has been demolished. Here you can find significant collections of lace, silverware, Dutch wall tiles and furniture. The old gatehouse was used as a county gaol up until the First World War. A remarkable thing you can find in some of the preserved prison cells is the graffiti of that time, which has been carved into the wooden walls.

MØGELTØNDER

The cobbled street Slotsgade is rightly called Denmark's most beautiful village street with its 250 listed thatched houses, many of which with bay windows according to the tradition in Schleswig. The actual town was originally a harbour square, but already in the 13th century the fairway shoaled, and a new harbour square flourished where the market town of Tønder is situated today.

The church of Møgeltønder is another of the town's sights. The rich furnishings include many wall paintings from approximately 1550, whereas the pictures in the rood arch date back as far as around 1275. Denmark's oldest church organ still in use from 1679 plays beautifully at all religious ceremonies and creates a special atmosphere, while you look at the gothic triptych, the great baroque pulpit or the Romanesque baptismal font. The steeple served for almost 100 years until 1628 as an important navigation mark, until a Christmas storm blew down the spire. A new one was soon erected, but to the great disappointment of the sailors it was 15 metres shorter than the previous one.

Schackenborg Palace (Schackenborg Slot) is situated at the end of Slotsgade, and its history dates back to 1233, when the castle belonged to the bishop of Ribe. Originally the palace was called Møgeltønderhus, but when it was bestowed on the general Hans Schack by the Crown in 1661, it got its present name and has remained in the family ever since. The present main building is from approximately 1750. The palace is closed to the public, but the lovely palace park is open in the daytime.

In 1978 the childless Hans Schack donated the entire Schackenborg Palace to prince Joachim, who took over the castle at the age of 24 in 1993 and lives here now with princess Alexandra. The palace has thus returned to the Crown after having been owned by the same noble family for over 300 years.

Schackenborg

RIBE

Ribe is unquestionably the oldest city in Denmark and it contains more market town charm with well-preserved streets than any other town on the west coast. The city's history dates back to the 8th century and numerous medieval buildings and cobbled streets dominate the look of the city. Its situation close to the Jutland Wadden Sea (Vadehavet) with the river Ribe _ as a natural traffic artery created a settlement already in the Iron Age, which slowly developed into a merchant and cathedral city.

The environment surrounding the river has a special atmosphere, where cows still graze on the flat stretch of meadowland all the way up to the old part of the city. The wharf has been beautifully preserved with its cobbled quay, where only few boats dock, among others the liner Riberhus, which in the summer sail on the river along the beautiful and singular marshland behind the dikes.

As a memory of centuries' battles against the sea, the flood column (Stormflodssøjlen) at the centre of the harbour quay (Skibsbroen) shows a number of rings with years placed around the column for every time the sea washed masses of water through dikes and rivers over Ribe during storms. The top metal ring shows a height of nearly 6 metres over the normal water level as a memory of the worst flood in 1634, where thousands of lives were lost to the sea, and great areas of land were lost for ever. The first dike was built in this century, but even in 1976 and 1981 the sea threatened the old market town again.

Ribe has miraculously survived several catastrophes, which so many other towns have suffered under. Floods, fires and wars have only to a small extent affected the idyllic, old town, the centre of which contains over 100 listed buildings, of which as many as 25 are of class A. In addition the streets have a 17th century appearance, and on summer nights it is a special experience to see and hear the old watchman walk through the historic streets while he sings the famous watchman's songs.

Originally the cathedral was situated at the highest point of the city, but over the last 800 years the weight of the heavy walls have made the church sink several metres into the soft marsh soil, and today it appears in a pit with steps around it. The church was begun in 1117, but it probably was not continued until after a town fire in 1176. The impressive high citizens' tower, also called the tocsin tower (Stormklokketårnet), was erected some time in the 14th century and it was later fitted as a watch tower. There are extensive views of the marshland from up here, if you feel like climbing the 243 steps. Inside the cathedral offers numerous experiences in the high bright interior. Among the many personalities who are connected with the church are the Lutheran Hans Tavsen, who became a bishop in 1541, and the hymn writer Hans Adolf Brorson, who was bishop from 1741.

RØMØ

The peculiar tidal flats of the Jutland Wadden Sea, a natural area which is completely unique in Europe, is situated between the coast of Southern Jutland and the actual North Sea. With the tide having a range of 1.70 metres an enormous larder is created for millions of birds in the spring and autumn, when the sea lays bare its mud surfaces which are so rich in food twice every 24 hours.

On the Wadden Sea island Rømø, the southernmost of the three largest islands, you will find the widest sand beach in Europe, which measures 1 km at normal water level. On hot summer days, when the white beach is crowded with tourists from far away the beach seethes with activity. One weekend every year there is a kite festival and the sky is filled with entertaining, colourful kites.

Picturesque red farms with beautiful, well decorated entrances are scattered over Rømø. The population has always counted on the sea and in the 18th century the fishermen went all the way to the Arctic Ocean to hunt whales. For many people the whales became a very rewarding source of income, and on the north side of the island you will find the fine Commander's House (Kommandørgård) which has been converted into a museum with fine Dutch tiles on the walls, and the beautiful furnishings which were typical for the time have been preserved. This is what one of the 50 whaler homes on Rømø of that time looked like.

FANØ

The northernmost of the three Wadden Sea islands is called Fanø, and is the only one of them which has an actual town. Already in 1891 the North Sea bath Fanø Vesterhavsbad, was established as one of the first fashionable holiday resorts of the bourgeoisie. The 200 metre wide sand beach was attractive and the Copenhageners flocked to Fanø. Today the hard beach is passable for cars as is also the case on Rømø.

From olden days fishing and trading with Norway, Holland and England have been of great importance. Trade really got going in 1741, when the inhabitants managed to buy the island free of the old tenure with Riberhus Ladegård, and a significant part of the production of the special Jutland pottery from the Varde area was shipped from Fanø. In 1859 Fanø reached the status of having the second largest merchant fleet in the country.

The old streets of Nordby are still idyllic with the characteristic red-washed 19th century houses. Fanø Museum is located on the road Skolevej and it displays old furniture, tools and utensils which reflect life on the island 200 years ago. The maritime museum and costume collection (Fanø Skibsfart- og Dragtsamling) which is located on the main street (Hovedgaden) shows the impressive Fanø costumes, which, with their special headgear, are among the most famous costumes in Denmark. Also the unspoiled village environment of Sønderho on the south of the island offers a lot of charm with its small, twisted streets and paths.

BLÅVANDSHUK

With violent yet at the same time gentle nature, the west coast of Denmark speaks to the hearts of many tourists. In the summer the weather out here close to the North Sea changes between sunshine and clouds with cool sea fog, which in the morning and evening hours sometimes spreads out its white cloak over the magnificent sand dunes with heather moors and pine forests. Most people only know the west coast of Jutland from their experiences on the white beaches in the summer when the tourist season attracts families of happy holiday-makers who are eager to go swimming from far away. But the storms of the autumn and winter soon transform Western Jutland into a deserted area, where you more easily realise the great distances between farms and villages.

Blåvandshuk, the westernmost point in Denmark has been known and feared by sailors ever since sailing ships started their traffic along the west coast. The 40 km long reef, Horns Rev, stretches dangerously straight out from the projection (Hukket) as the longest reef on the west coast. Precisely these conditions have created special currents which wash up amber and other things on the beach. When the winds come from the right direction "amber fever" breaks out, and attracts people who then stand together in groups of up to 100 in the cast-up zone, while the "professionals" drive along the beach on mopeds on their hunt for the big lumps of amber.

In 1888 the first lighthouse, Blåvandshuk Fyr, was erected to guide the ships, and 12 years later it was converted to the square giant we know today. With its 42.6 metres the lighthouse is among the highest on the West Coast, only surpassed by Skagen Fyr.

HVIDE SANDE

The large fishing port which was established at the same time as the large lock system in 1931 is crammed with pale blue fishing vessels. You can experience a special atmosphere here when the smell of salt water and tar is mixed with the sound of fishing vessels and the screams of the seagulls. Hvide Sande must stand as the epitome of west-coast culture with more than 200 fishing vessels, ice factories, boatbuilder's yards and not least the popular auction hall, in which a large number of fishermen who are eager to buy and curious tourists gather every morning.

The beautiful old museum farm, Abelines Gård, is situated with the fjord and the sea as its closest neighbours just south of Hvide Sande in the centre of a dune tongue. The four-winged dune farm was built by the receiver of wrecks in 1871. His son who took over the farm after him, died already in 1904 and left his wife Abeline with five children. Abeline continued to run the farm for 53 years, until she herself had to give up in 1957 and died at the age of 87. In 1974 the worn-down farm was restored and converted into a museum. An attempt has been made to preserve the interiors unchanged from the time of Abeline, and many local people have supplemented the museum's collections of old things.

Abelines Gård

Viborg Domkirke

VIBORG

Viborg is situated in the heart of Jutland. From here there is an equal distance to the waters surrounding Jutland. Fertile meadows and fields, thriving beech forests and a magnificent hilly landscape with deep lakes characterise the highland of central Jutland. This is how far the ice reached before it withdrew northwards 15,000 years ago and created the hilly landscape we know today.

West of Viborg the soil has a high calcium content. For almost 1000 years hundreds of kilometres of tunnel were dug and thereby created an extensive network to collect the lime for buildings. In this underworld there are many stories of the robbers and murderers of olden times who took refuge down here.

Viborg Cathedral rises high above the city and the lake as the pride of the city. The present buildings are a free reconstruction from 1865 of the original medieval church of Viborg. Once inside the church, you will be surprised by the impressive decoration of walls and ceilings, which was mainly done by Joakim Skovgaard one hundred years ago.

HJERL HEDE

The Old Village on Hjerl Hede, a wonderful open-air museum with many old farms which have been taken down all over the country and carefully rebuilt stone by stone, is situated west of Viborg. The oldest house is actually the oldest farm in Denmark from 1530 and it was moved here from the village of Vinkel in Central Jutland. In addition an Iron Age house and various pre-historic settlements have been reconstructed, and here a number of people are dressed and live like people did several thousands years ago. In the summer the Danish peasant life comes alive with costumes and performances so that you can gain an impression of a village community in the 19th century.

Not very far from Hjerl Hede there is an exciting, well-preserved medieval castle, Spøttrup. Only few castles are surrounded with so much mystery which appeals to your fantasy.

Spøttrup

THE SILKEBORG LAKES

The Silkeborg Lakes (Silkeborg-Søerne) in Central and Eastern Jutland constitute the largest lake district of Denmark with a wonderful combination of forest-clad uplands and long glittering lakes. In the summer months the old excursion boats come alongside the quays along the lakes from Silkeborg to Ry. The best known boat is the oldest paddle steamer in the country, Hjejlen, which was built in 1861. Here a good deal of nostalgia has been preserved, when Hjejlen starts its journey with smoke and steam towards yet another sight, Himmelbjerget.

In the lake area between Silkeborg and Horsens you will find the three highest points in Denmark close to one another. Ejer Bavnehøj was regarded as the highest point for many years with its 171 metres above sea level, but envious peasants from the neighbourhood built a small artificial hill on top of their Yding Skovhøj, so that it reached a height of 173 metres. More recent fine measurements show, however, that Møllehøj is the highest, real hilltop, only a few centimetres higher than Ejer Bavnehøj.

However, the hill that has become famous is a completely different one. It is Himmelbjerget with its height of as little as 147 metres, but because of the great difference in height down to the lake Julsø it seems more impressive. The 24-metre high tower, which was erected in 1874 as a monument to Frederik VII, stands high as landmark for the Silkeborg Lakes. From up here there is a remarkable view over the entire lake landscape in clear weather.

ÅRHUS

At the end of many of the fjords of East Jutland you will find some of the largest market towns of Jutland with flourishing industry and a charming trading environment in the shopping streets and shopping centres of the towns. At the Kattegat coast lies Århus, the second largest city in Denmark and the capital of Jutland, with approximately a quarter of a million inhabitants. The city has an abundance of sights and has made its mark in its competition with Copenhagen on the cultural scene.

The Concert Hall (Musikhuset) is the cultural centre of Århus, and since it was erected in 1982 it has been the centre of many great, international musical events and exhibitions.

Århus Cathedral Århus Domkirke) in the centre of Store Torv is the longest church in the country at 93 metres, and it has more frescos than any other Danish church. The unusual interiors of the church exceed those of most other churches in age, decorations and size. The organ alone is from 1730 and with its 6,352 pipes it is in a league of its own and the largest in the country. A couple of kilometres south of the city you will find a large green area. This is where Tivoli Friheden can be found, the counterpart of the Zealanders' Tivoli Gardens, although it is more modest in size. In the forest the white Marselisborg Palace (Marselisborg Slot) is situated, and at only 100 years old it is the youngest royal palace in the country. The royal family use this palace for periods as a summer residence. Further down the coast towards the south you will find the manor Moesgaard, the farm buildings of which have been converted into a prehistoric museum.

Århus Domkirke

Marselisborg Slot

THE OLD TOWN

One of the greatest sights in _rhus is undoubtedly the market town museum The Old Town (Den gamle By). Here you will find around 60 well-preserved half-timbered houses and farms from the period between 1570 and 1900. They have been carefully moved here from all over the country and both rebuilt and refitted with furnishings which are typical for the time. In the town you can experience a well-established street environment with working workshops, shops, a school and a theatre. The market town museum thus creates a perfect picture of life in Danish towns throughout 300 years for both poor and rich. If you take a stroll in the museum town you feel as though you have been carried back to a time where artistic taste and craftsmanship met on an unsurpassed level.

EBELTOFT

The peninsula of Djursland stretches towards the east out into the Kattegat just north of Århus. Here the scenery is more beautiful than anywhere else in Eastern Jutland, especially the hilly landscape of Mols Bjerge towards the south provides an unforgettable view in clear weather from its highest point which is 137 metres above sea level. In the distance you can make out the castle ruin, Kalø Slotsruin, which was built back in the Middle Ages. With walls which were three metres thick, it was a strong castle which lasted for 300 years. In the basement was the notorious dungeon where among others the Swedish king Gustav Vasa was once imprisoned.

The greatest sight on Djursland is the old market town of Ebeltoft with its many well-preserved half-timbered houses and its idyllic streets. Here you will encounter one picturesque image of the town after the other. The old town hall from 1576 with its pretty belfry and the old canons in front of it is situated in the town square. This is where the watchmen start their round in the summer at sunset. Today the town hall houses Ebeltoft Folk Museum (Ebeltoft Folkemuseum).

Another of Ebeltoft's attractions is the newly restored frigate, Fregatten Jylland, which as the longest wooden ship in the world participated in the battle at Helgoland in 1864. A visit here takes you back to the golden age of sail with all its charm.

Fregatten Jylland

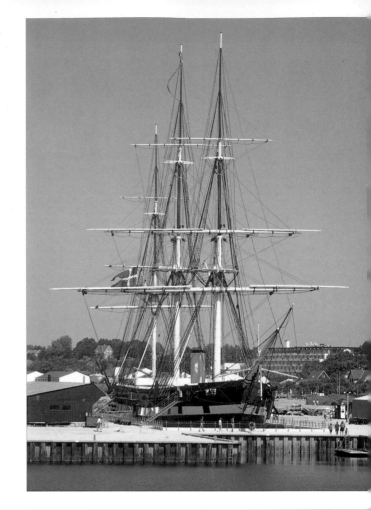

Aalborgtårnet

AALBORG

From olden days Aalborg has been the "capital" of Northern Jutland with its good location inside the fjord, Limfjorden. Until the end of the 18th century, it was the second largest city in Denmark and today it is the fourth largest, surpassed by Copenhagen, _rhus and Odense. The city's large white cathedral, St Botolph's Cathedral (Skt. Budolfi), is named after an English saint and constitutes a centre in Aalborg. The most remarkable thing about the church is the rich interior from many different ages. Aalborg Castle (Aalborg Slot) from approximately 1540 is situated close to the port, a white manor-like building with red timber frames which was established as a substitute for the fortress Aalborghus. The Municipality is located here, but there is access to the county council hall and you can have a look down into a dark dungeon.

The modern white North Jutland Art Museum (Nordjyllands Kunstmuseum) is a contrast to the old bourgeois neighbourhood behind the church with twisted alleys and Jens Bang's Stone House (Jens Bangs Stenhus) from the 17th century. The buildings of the art museum are themselves works of art, and inside you will find a fine collection of international art from the 20th century, where among other things the works of art of the Cobra group dominate.

Many are not interested in this type of sight, however. Instead they come for a visit to the street Jomfru Ane Gade, which is characterised by cosy pubs with live music and dancing until the early morning.

Budolfi Kirke

Jens Bangs stenhus

Jomfru Ane Gade

SKAGEN

The northernmost town in Denmark, Skagen, was discovered as a holiday resort at the end of the 19th century, when the fashionable bourgeoisie of Copenhagen settled in the wonderful surroundings. In the old part of the town the characteristic yellow-washed houses dominate with white-painted roof ridges, and by the charming fishing port you can see the picturesque red warehouses from 1907, in which there is always lively activity in the summer..

You can go out on the tip of Skagen, the so-called Grenen, with the tractor-bus Sandormen and see where the two seas the Kattegat and the Skagerrak meet with large, pointed waves, which can reach many metres in height during a storm. South of the town you will find the landmark of Skagen, the Sand-covered Church (Den tilsandede Kirke). The church was originally the longest in North Jutland, but the devastating sand drift over the years closed the entire entrance several times and a couple of hundred years ago the church was torn down. Only the tower has been preserved as a memory of the sand drift and as a navigation mark for the ship traffic. The sea around Skagen has always been feared by sailors, and a total of four lighthouses from different periods are placed around Skagen. The oldest is the bascule light from 1560, which consisted of an iron basket with burning firewood which was raised 25 metres up in the dark period of winter.

The unique light in Skagen has brought many great painters to the town. The combination of sea on both sides and dry, clear air from the Norwegian mountains created the special atmosphere which made great personalities settle up here at a time when innkeeping was still scarce. Martinus Rørbye was the first painter to observe the peculiarity of the place in 1833, and he became known for the painting "Strandscene på gamle Skagen med et optrækkende uvejr" (beach scene on old Skagen with a storm gathering) from 1834. But Skagen did not become internationally known until the great names of the Danish Golden Age such as Anna and Michael Ancher, P.S. Krøyer, Holger Drachmann, Karl Madsen and Christian Krohg settled here and introduced a new era within Danish art history from the 1870s to the turn of the century with their pictures of the fishing hamlets and the scenes which took place here which were so characteristic of the time. Skagen has a lot of museums. Skagen's Museum on the road Brøndumsvej was established by a number of personalities in 1908 and was later expanded three times. The museum exhibits more than 1000 paintings, sketches, sculptures and handicrafts by Skagen artists from the period 1830-1930. In "Villa Pax" on the road Hans Baghsvej you will find the house of Anna and Michael Ancher, which shows the home of the artist couple after the careful restoration in 1964. A fourth art museum is Axel Lind's Grenen Museum, where changing exhibitions show modern art.

Den tilsandede Kirke

BORNHOLM

Bornholm is situated out in the Baltic Sea right between Sweden and Poland as the easternmost of the largest Danish islands, almost 150 km from the rest of Denmark. Bornholm differs significantly from the rest of the country with its characteristic nature and peculiar weather. Bornholm is known as the sunshine island with clean air and bright light. Over here the trees burst into leaf one week later, and spring is often cool and foggy because of the cold Baltic Sea. In return the late summer is warm and mild for a longer time than in the rest of Denmark.

With ferry connections to three countries there is easy access for tourists to the "Pearl of the Baltic Sea". Here the steep cliff coasts toward the west and north form a sharp contrast to the flat sand beach with the white dunes on the south coast, but here and there all over the island the bedrock sticks out like great boulders, and Bornholm is the only place in Denmark where this can be seen.

Among the most impressive parts of the cliff is Jon's Chapel (Jons Kapel), which is a 40 metre high free-standing coastal cliff. According to the legend a monk by the name of Jon, who preached from a ledge of the cliff, lived here. One of the greatest sights of Bornholm, Hammershus, is situated further up the west coast, which after a long glorious period of 500 years from 1255 gradually became a ruin. The castle grounds are quite large and cover an area of approximately 3500 m². In addition to many hundreds of metres of ring walls of up to 9 metres in height, a couple of towers have been partly preserved.

Jons Kapel

Hammershus

Nylars Kirke

Rønne ↓ →

A particular feature of Bornholm is the peculiar round churches from the 12th century, which with their walls of several metres in thickness partly served as medieval fortresses. Fishing is the one great occupation on Bornholm, and this has made the island famous far and wide with its delicious smoked herring and salmon. Here and there on the island you will see the characteristic smokehouses, where the fish hang in rows and are heated over the embers of alderwood.

In the centre of the island lies the great forest of Almindingen which with its area of 25 km² is the third largest forest in Denmark. Ponds and little lakes alternate with deep gorges in a unique atmosphere which without a doubt makes the area among the most beautiful in the country. From the tower on the highest point of the island, Rytterknægten which is situated 162 metres above sea level, there is a wonderful view of most of the island in clear weather.

Christiansø, the main island in the easternmost group of islands in Denmark, Ertholmene, is an experience in itself. The small fortress island was of great importance in the 17th and 18th centuries, but today the old defence walls and fortress towers only serve the interests of the tourists.